DOES THIS MASK MAKE ME LOOK FAT?

And Other Poems From The Lockdown

By

Tomás Romero

Moonbeast Media, June 2021

ISBN: 978-1-7361949-3-5 (ebook)
ISBN: 978-1-7361949-2-8 (print)

Formatting by Polgarus Studio
www.polgarusstudio.com

Copy edited by Stephanie Parent
www.stephanieparentediting.blogspot.com

Cover design/layout by Rachel Kerns

Author photo by Ryan Romero
www.ryanromerovideo.com

Author Website
www.tomasnromero.wordpress.com

Printed in the United States of America

For the Mardi Gras queen of London, Ontario.
Long may she reign…

CONTENTS

INTRODUCTION

Any way you look at it, 2020 was flaming insanity on a stick. And though some people have taken to calling it "the year that wasn't," I prefer to think of 2020 as a year that was just a little too "extra" for its own good. Like five really shitty years rolled into one or a long, sad, totally bonkers Kevin Costner movie that just would not end. Like *The Postman*, *Waterworld* or fucking *Message in a Bottle.*

And then, even when it did end and hope dared to rear its withered, battle-weary head in 2021, everything went to shit again at the Capitol. Yeah, roller coasters got nothing on 2020, baby. As if the pandemic wasn't enough, the past year and a half also offered us searing racial, social and political unrest, incalculable human and economic loss, a mental health crisis for the ages, and some seriously end of days-ish ecological calamities as well.

It didn't matter where you lived or worked or how much money you had or didn't have, literally no one was left untouched or unchanged by the bleak, never-ending shitstorm that was daily life on planet Earth in 2020.

But, that doesn't mean it was all bad.

I don't quote Scripture often, if ever, but that part in Romans about suffering producing perseverance, character and hope is kinda spot-on. If you ask me, anyone who has lived through these truly strange days—especially kids and tweens—will surely be stronger and more resourceful because of it. Maybe not right away, or even a few years down the line, but, eventually. In time. I hope.

And I'm not just talking about mastering their banana bread and sourdough starter games either. I'm talking about a global, post-pandemic glow up where grit, kindness and straight-up badassery are the real new normal.

During lockdown we learned how to live, work and even love differently, and I remain ever hopeful that humankind will come out the other side of this ongoing madness better, wiser and more empathetic and connected than ever before. Or, at the very least, open to the possibility that this moment can effect lasting change in the way we interact with one another and the world around us.

I know that might sound a bit sunny and optimistic—especially considering the current state of the world—but if my long, anxiety-filled "gap year" has taught me anything, it's that hope really can spring eternal. Even during a global pandemic.

Peace-
TR

AUTHOR'S NOTE

The poems included in this collection were all written during the COVID-19 lockdown from March 2020 through June of 2021. I had originally planned to organize them in chronological order or divided by seasons or possibly into categories like home, work, life and school. But the fact that the pandemic chucked all those elements into an ice-crushing blender on high daily made it difficult to decide which poems should go where.

So, in the end, I elected to organize this collection into loosely organized "chapters" based on some of the new, pandemic-tastic slang terms we've all come to know and love/hate during lockdown. Like the old-school mix tapes of my analog youth, some poems are happy, some are sad, some are both at once and some should probably include a trigger warning—particularly if you ate, drank or smoked too much during lockdown or have ever worked as a Walmart greeter.

I'm just sorry I couldn't find a way to fit my favorite pandemic term, cluttercore, in here somewhere too. Not just because it so aptly describes the chaos and physical clutter we all dealt with during lockdown, but because it also perfectly encapsulates the emotional clutter so many us struggled, and continue to struggle with, as well.

Either way, thanks for picking up my book.

THE POEMS

THE FIRST WAVE

SPRING BREAK(down)

It was Friday the 13th
a few days past a big full moon
When the world took a strange turn
from which no one was immune

Like a horrible spring break
one that lasted a full year
Filled with strife and killer cops
senseless death and so much fear

We won't really know what hit us
until it's in the rearview mirror
So buckle up, sweet girl
because the free fall starts right here

EVERYTHING'S GONE GREEN

Coyotes rule the canyons
bears and bobcats too
Raccoons and skunks are back en vogue
at swimming pools near you

Rats and crows are branching out
from dumpsters in the alleys
And snakes are everywhere you look
when hiking in the valleys

The smog burns off each day by noon
the skies have such a glow
And traffic is a midcentury dream
20 minutes, anywhere you go

Everything's gone green again
but daily life is still damn scary
So I go green a lot these days
with buds that are quite hairy

PANDEMICA ROSE

Cookie had been journaling
since she was sweet sixteen
But she found her true life's calling
while under quarantine

She started writing stories
about her family and her friends
And a world that was unraveling
and fraying at the ends

Her pain spilled out upon the page
in all its purple prose
And she took on a cool pen name,
Miss Pandemica Rose

Her blog posts soon went viral
her Insta stories too
As the world embraced the sister
with the faded Prince tattoo

Her voice was raw and clear
she made her feelings known
This mother wasn't playing
her fucks to give were gone

And when school started up again
online only, in the fall
Pandemica kept on writing
in the kitchen down the hall

Her kids and husband stood in awe
of the force she had become
And Pandemica Rose dazzled us all
with her writerly aplomb

FINE

I'm fine, he said
just a little stressed
As he fed the kids breakfast
and got them all dressed

Logging into work
his new daily grind
Trying so hard to
quiet his mind

But he wasn't fine
or just a little stressed
Unwashed, unwell
and barely dressed

This is what losing your mind must feel like,
he thought

And as his wife and kids online schooled
down the hall
He sipped his beer breakfast
and dreamt of the fall

But one long year later
he realized at dawn
That the fall he had longed for
was already gone

SOURDOUGH STARTER SANDI

Secret Smoker Sandi
switched to sourdough by spring
And made whipping up starter
her new pandemic thing

She baked bread for her neighbors
she baked bread for her friends
She even started selling it
and the orders never end

And though she put on weight
and saved loads of money on her cigs
Sandi missed her secret smoking
and her alone time sans her kids

And as she stood there baking
in the chaos of her kitchen
The thought of smoking freely
set her smoking fingers twitching

So Sandi started home deliveries
to customers near and far
And caught up on her smoking
on the highway in her car

YOU'RE NO MATT DAMON

"It's just like that movie," I said to my kid
as we all hunkered down in the early days of COVID

"Yeah, except it's way more boring," she grumbled
"And you're no Matt Damon!"

She was right
and that was a good one
But I still took her iPad away

CORONA BOB

Corona Bob's hair got long
in lockdown real quick
He started out as Neo
and ended up like fat John Wick

His wife and daughter liked it
but Bob liked it even more
He hadn't worn his hair that long
since 1994!

Embracing his new grungy vibe
Bob dug up his old flannels
Which hadn't fit since Y2K
when TV still had channels

So Bob donated his old grunge gear
and bought new shirts online
Some even came with matching masks
which suited him just fine

And though Corona Bob's Corona bob
was soon grayer than his beard
He rocked his new grunge grandpa look
straight through to the new year

But when Bob started looking
more like *Twin Peaks* Bob instead
His wife stepped in and cut that shit
straight off his grungy head

SCREEN TIME

Worrying about my kid's screen time
feels a little bit like worrying about head lice
or getting good seats at the fucking talent show

Screen time is just called time at our house these days

WORDS WITH FRIENDS

You ain't even gotta be my friend
I will literally take words with anyone right now
I don't need to win
I just want to feel normal. Connected.

Not. Alone.

That said, a triple word score today
would be fucking glorious

No pressure

ESSENTIAL

SMIZE

"We'll have to smile with our eyes more,
like Tyra Banks used to do,"
said Lupe's boss at the start of her shift

But with her hours reduced
sick parents at home
And her kids struggling online and adrift

Lupe was in no mood to fucking smize

In fact, she frowned even harder
beneath her branded grocery store clerk mask
Her newfound suit of armor

ESSENTIAL WORKER ELLA

Sometimes
After working a 12-hour shift
Six or seven days in a row
In cobbled together, raggedy-ass PPE
With no sleep
No breaks
No time to even think
With death hovering over everything she does
And everyone she touches
Every damn day
Like a fucking Dementor's kiss

Nurse Ella doesn't feel so essential

Undervalued
Underpaid
Overworked
Overwhelmed

The clapping and tributes are lovely
Same with the treats and the cards

But what Ella really wants
Essentially
Are a couple of fucking days off in a row

FAB FLIGHT FREDDY

Back in flight attendant school
he was the brightest star
Fit, fabulous and friendly
Freddy's skills would take him far

He worked the LA-Honolulu route
for almost thirty years
And lived for his friends like family
and fine, Aussie craft beers

But despite all his best efforts
he was one of the first to die
Felled by COVID pneumonia
he was gone by mid-July

His cabin crew sometimes still feel him
his magic mana in the air
Taking wing across the ocean
with his Fab Flight Freddy flair

CURBSIDE PICKUP

They saw each other once a week
as she placed the order in her trunk

Smizing through the driver's side window
contactless crushing, who'd have thunk?

By the third month in they grew bolder
with her window rolled down just a crack

Chatting through their masks about music
movies, TV shows and snacks

But it was their shared love of Doritos
paired with a fine Mango White Claw

That sparked true romance between them
and sealed the deal from afar

She also tipped really well, so, that definitely helped

GUESTHOUSE

Dr. A lived in his guesthouse
in the backyard behind the pool

Separate from his wife and kids
to keep them safe, healthy and cool

They didn't see each other much
because Dr. A worked long-ass hours

But they'd leave him gifts outside his door
candy, beer and sometimes flowers

And when he got vaccinated
Dr. A moved back inside

Held his family close to him
and broke straight down and cried

It was a good day

SALSA BRAVA

Salsa Victoria
was born Victor Camino
in a crowded apartment
just north of Encino

A plus-size drag diva
Salsa ruled the roost
At a dive bar in Pacoima
called The Caboose

She wasn't the skinniest girl
up on stage
But she gave damn good face
and did not show her age

The tips weren't half bad
at her shows on the weekend
But when COVID hit hard
Salsa's troubles began

The Caboose closed its doors
and she couldn't find work
Even a straight gig
as a cashier or a clerk

No PUA flowed her way
or old school UI
Thank God for the Del Taco
drive-thru nearby

Salsa worked the night shift
with her usual flair
Rocking a pink sequined mask
with fierceness to spare

THE GREETER

Esme Watson worked at Walmart
an old-school greeter from way back
Known for her big-ass smile
and bigger hair deep, dark and black

She'd won a Shining Star award
and greeted presidents and kings
But after the first mask mandate
she saw some crazy things

In June they simply cursed at her
by August they were spitting
On Boxing Day some dick threw punches
which seemed perfectly fitting

Her boss asked her to switch it up
and maybe work somewhere inside
But Esme'd been a frontline greeter
since 1985

So she stuck proudly to her post
enforced mask wearing at the door
Until a freedom loving anti-masker
one day knocked her to the floor

That was a deal breaker for Esme
who simply wasn't paid enough
To combat COVID deniers
with a penchant for getting rough

So she transferred to the deli
and spit in their soup instead
They never knew what hit them
but their former greeter surely did

THE PERMANENCE OF STONE

Milo ran a rock store
at the far end of the earth
In a dusty roadside townsite
a hundred miles outside of Perth

Isolation didn't phase him
nor the pandemic or the fires
He and his rocks had seen much worse
and times much more stark and dire

Milo's tourmaline was timeless
same with his agates and rose quartz
This was not their first pandemic
and they simply stayed the course

Milo didn't fair as well
and died one warm fall day
Leaving his empire of rocks
to his family far away

"What the fuck are we gonna do with all these rocks?" they wondered

THE BIG BLUR

FIVE-STAR ISLAND (ANIMAL CROSSING)

I haven't had a writing gig
since just past Halloween
But I have a five-star island
that is beautiful and clean

Nobody ever dies here
not even the fish
And when the sky is full of stars
I close my eyes and make a wish

I know the real world is dark
and scary as all fuck
But this crazy game just saved my soul
all hail, tanuki Nook!

CRAZY CAT LADY POLLY

Crazy Cat Lady Polly
was at the end of her rope
Furloughed in May
she was anxious and broke

Her unemployment checks
kept her barely afloat
As she quarantined with her cats
and her trusty remote

She watched every film
Ethan Hawke ever made
And read, knit and baked
and made fresh lemonade

Her friends porch-dropped treats
and they bartered with food
And her five crazy cats
often lightened the mood

But cats were poor stand-ins
for her friends and her work
And though she hated to sound
like an ungrateful jerk

Polly couldn't wait to get the fuck out of her stanky-ass apartment
And she was pretty sure her cats felt the same way

Especially Gattaca, that cat was a dick!

CELEBRITY DOOM SCROLLING

I was not an *US* or *People* reader
even in normal times
But during the pandemic
that shit was my total lifeline

Forget *The Bachelor* wannabes
I wanted to see some stars
Masked up and jogging with their dogs,
schlepping groceries to their cars!

Taylor hiking with her new dude
Dakota Johnson at Erewhon
Megan Fox shopping for kale
and Reese or Gwyneth on a run

This became my new obsession
when the real news was just too bleak
Pics of stars looking like crap
soothed my soul a bit each week

It made me feel less alone
and part of the same strange hell
Doom scrolling paparazzi pics
is lame, I know, oh well…

THE FLOOR STORE

When our orders come in
from Costco and Target
On the floor by the door
is where most of them get set

Of course, we wipe the shit down
that we need right away
But the rest can detox
for a couple of days

And though we used to think colds
and flus were so scary
Now it's the fomites
that make us most wary

It looks kinda crazy
but who cares anymore
The world at your feet
in our fugly floor store

BETTY'S WORK-LIFE BALANCE

Raising two kids alone
Betty strove for work-life balance
But working from home now
made her miss her work drive silence

Telecommuting and homeschooling
were harder than they sounded
And she ended every day
overworked and fucking hounded

Dinnertime sucked ass too
and she was sick of doing dishes
And if a genie showed up now
she'd need a lot more than three wishes

But if she had just three
number one would surely be
One night without her shitheads
alone with her TV

Come to think of it, wishes two and three
would probably be more of the same

Oh how Betty longed for those imbalanced days of old!

GAME NIGHT ETERNAL

Phase 10 and UNO Flip!
Monopoly and Clue
Games kept us sane, man
they were our COVID glue

When the screens burned our eyes
and doom scrolling got old
We'd gather round the table
and feel better threefold

Keeping a diary of our wins
our losses and sweeps
With a bright rainbow pen
we were playing for keeps!

And when all this ends
and real life resumes
I'll long for these nights
locked down in these rooms

Game night eternal
game night forever
I'll miss these strange days
and all their sweet splendor

FARMER'S DAUGHTER

The Farmer's Daughter grew up
in a town far away
On a rambling old farm
surrounded by hay

She raised horses and pigs
and showed them at fairs
And sewed, knit and baked
with unusual flair

She loved music and art
and movies and books
But wanted more than the farm
so to the city she took

San Francisco and LA
were more to her liking
And she ruled her new realms
like a strong, silent Viking

And when The Great Pause hit
and the world went to hell
She rallied her family
and rode out the swell

Her husband and kid
went a bit COVID crazy
But she was undaunted
and slayed dragons daily

She made masks and bread
and her own sourdough starter
And nurtured new sources
to trade with and barter

Crafty and resourceful,
whip-smart and kind
She kept her family and friends
from losing their minds

Her father would be proud
of the woman she became
And surely take delight
in her well-earned nickname

HAIRCUT

I learned to cut hair this year
and I'm actually not half bad
YouTube clips and fancy scissors
turned me from dad to rad

Clear plastic rubber bands helped too
and my trusty comb made out of wood
I'm not so great at straight lines
but my choppy bobs are good

And if I really fuck it up
it grows back pretty quick
Or I can shave it off completely
like some New Wave rocker chick

Either way, they can't beat my prices!

LATE-NIGHT FILM SCHOOL

Movies at midnight
pancakes at three
We'd sit huddled together
watching TV

Billy Wilder and Hitchcock
Valley Girl and Truffaut
We paired Corman with De Sica
to really change up our flow

West Side Story and *Fame*
The Red Shoes and *Charade*
Both Hepburns one week
and man, "Moon River" slayed!

Natalie Wood broke our hearts
in *Splendor in the Grass*
And *The Breakfast Club*
knocked my sweet girl on her ass

Film school was in session
all night long with my kid
As we rode out the darkness
of the summer COVID

QUARANTINE 15

MIRTH & HOPELESSNESS

Twin sisters of the lockdown
the yin and the yang duet
Of months spent living indoors
filled with laughter and regret

One day mirth might loom larger
with board games, beer and chatter
Followed by hopeless nights
where nothing seemed to matter

Facebook, Zoom and alcohol
helped balance these two extremes
But lasting peace could never spring
from binging shows and memes

One day I hope the two might find
a happy middle ground
But until they do I'll eat my feelings,
pound by merry pound

GROUNDED

He doesn't get out much these days
and the nights are longer still
His Postmates side hustle on pause
until the world becomes more chill

He doesn't really miss the gig
but the smells do haunt him so
Falafels and fragrant Thai food
greasy chips, chow fun to go

Pancakes and Tommy Burgers too
his car smelled like America
Moonlit rides with a pen and pad
the grounded dad bard of suburbia

Safe gig work gone for the duration
his fire still glows brightest at night
You won't see him in the daytime
but his vampire game is tight

REALITY SANDWICHES

It's hard to find bread
or turkey or meat
So reality sandwiches
are all we ever eat

Bologna and mayo
on stale tortillas of wheat
Or braunschweiger spread
that smells like dirty feet

Man, lockdown picnics blow!

DOOM DRINKING

Happy Hour Zooms are fun
especially when we're wasted

I think Kirkland brand Spiced Rum
is the best I've ever tasted

Or maybe that's the Kirkland
ready-to-drink Golden Margarita talking

Or the beer

Or the weed

Either way, thanks for the link
another chance to chat and drink!

HANGRY

Sometimes I get so hangry
I wanna burn all this shit down
The killer cops out on the street
the hipster hillbillies uptown

Our grifter president
The anti-maskers
Stimulus checks delayed
Our smoking neighbor from upstairs
Another sad, birthday parade

Burn.
It.
Down.

But instead of doing that
I eat some string cheese and a pickle
And I'm not hangry anymore
Just regular angry
And really fucking sad

So, I head back to bed
and dream of sushi

MIA'S STRESS CLEANSE DIET

Breaking in her Peloton
eating right and losing weight

Mia's stress cleanse diet
took her from a 12 to a size 8

At our last Zoom happy hour
she was the only one with her camera on

And.
She.
Looked.
Amazing.

Seriously, she was glowing from within
Hooray for fucking Mia

LAST NIGHT OUT

Noah ate at Denny's
for his kid's free b-day meal

While Mia had a Kobe steak
at that place that still serves veal

Kiki splurged on Shabu Shabu
Heather had Thai food and beer

And then we all never ate out again
for one whole fucking year

It doesn't matter where you ate
or at which buffet you grazed

That last time eating out
was like a ticker tape parade

Seriously, when this thing is over,
I might not ever cook again

ZOOMTOWN

ZOOM SHIRTS

Logan kept two Zoom shirts
neatly pressed right by his desk
Which he'd alternate with ties
and sometimes even a vest

He wore pants out of habit
for the first few weeks in spring
But comfy sweats or ratty boxers
soon became his Zoom time thing

"No one sees below my waist,"
he told his teacher wife and son
Who now keep Zoom shirts of their own
for distance learning fun

Their looks might not be sustainable
when things return to normal
But in the pants-free, barefoot era
Zoom shirts seem downright formal

AUDIBLE AIMEE

Aimee wasn't down with Zoom
and mostly kept her camera off
All through the summer and the fall
even with new guy, Geoff

But Geoff worked well with Aimee
and they made a killer team
Even before they ever met
IRL and not onscreen

So they agreed to work together
with their Zoom link on all day
Cameras off but mics on blast
side by side every weekday

They got to know each other's likes and loves
and shared their hopes and fears
While reinventing COVID office culture
for their co-workers and peers

They didn't fall in love or date
Aimee's gay and so is Geoff
But their arrangement saved them both
last year from loneliness and death

Plus they could totally talk shit about their boss all day
and no one could hear them but their dogs

VFFs

They all knew each other
long before the COVID times
But their bond was knit much closer
in weekly Zoom chats online

The group met every Thursday
to chat, knit and bitch
And help Penny perfect
her buttonhole stitch

Sometimes things got heated
and they shouted and quarreled
About the state of the country
and the fate of the world

But the kinship they crafted
while avoiding infection
Was stronger than all of their
Wi-Fi connections

And though they vowed to keep meeting
every week when things ended
Real life would soon find them
too overextended

So, they cherished their meetups,
those long, lazy nights spent online
Zooming in from four states
VFFs for all time

PURPLE TIER

ZOOM FUNERAL FOR A FRIEND

It started at noon
or so the link said
But live-streaming a funeral
kinda fucks with your head

So maybe it was later
Ella couldn't remember
She just knew it took place
in the dead of December

As an ICU nurse she'd
had several friends die
But this was her first streaming funeral
and Ella watched it and cried

Her goggles fogged over
beneath her plastic shield
And Ella was glad for the first time
that her face was concealed

So she watched till the end
in the break room by the lift
And then headed back out
to finish her shift

THE LONE SAILOR

The Lone Sailor set out to sea alone
long before the lockdown

Untethered
Unmoored
And thrice divorced
The King had long since stepped down

Awash in a sea of dark reds and whites
and malted barley's siren call
He'd run aground on jagged rocks
swift and steep his fall

But sometimes as he fell asleep
by his TV's warm, blue glow
He sailed off to happier shores
his old crew mates in tow

And oh, what adventures they had!

A COUCH TO DIE FOR

Septuagenarian Terri was
oh just so very
Locked down all alone
in her condo sanctuary

She wouldn't go shopping
to buy her own beans
Or TP or napkins
or anything in between

But when her furloughed neighbor
decided to move
In the first days of Corona
to a state far removed

He offered Miss Terri
his nearly new couch
He'd even deliver it,
that man was no slouch!

Social distancing be damned
he moved that couch in
And crossed Terri's threshold
with his buddy named Jim

Not a mask was in sight
who needed them here?
Terri'd known her nice neighbor
for over a year!

But Jim was the weak link
and got sick four days later
Ending up in a hospital
somewhere south of Decatur

Which frightened poor Terri
but did not dissuade her
From keeping a free couch
that might kill her later

So she wiped that thing down
with wipes reeking of bleach
Replaced all the pillows and
skipped off to the beach

UNSOLICITED ADVICE

Unsolicited advice
really gives me the feels
Especially about my kid

If you don't have skin in the game
or kids or tweens underfoot *(or even if you do!)*
Maybe just keep your quips hid

Seriously, the fucking world is on fire
Mind your business!

TIME

Time is all relative,
thought Rosemary Whitehead
As she lay all alone
in her nursing home bed

She hadn't been outside
for a month, maybe more
And only seen her grandkids
that one time through the door

And though the nurses came
every day with her meals
And she Facetimed with her kids
every week with such zeal

Time was testing
her old lady resolve
Every day, every hour
newfound ailments to solve

But Rosemary vowed
to push through the pain
And carry on till the world
was sunny again

She'd outlived two husbands,
breast cancer and the Blitz
Keeping calm was her jam
and time was her bitch

Sometimes, I think she'll outlive us all...

WINE FOR BREAKFAST

Kandy with a K
drank too much wine
Not only with breakfast
but any old time

She drank with her friends
via Zoom happy hours
And while tending her garden
with all its dead flowers

She drank through the summer
and she drank through the fall
And her fab liquid diet
was the envy of all

But deep down Kandy suffered
more than we knew
And her sunny worldview
became increasingly blue

She still ate healthy shit
but she drank too much wine
Which may have worked in the old days
before COVID time

But drinking and lockdown
did not pair so well
And her anxiety and despair
really put her through hell

One dark night Kandy cracked
and could not hit undo
And when her ex had the kids
from the rooftop she flew

ASYNCHRONOUS

TEACHER X

She gets up every morning
stumbles across her room
To flip on her glow up ring light
and get ready for her Zoom

Her toddler playing in the background
dogs and birds crazy sometimes
Teaching through a webcam
like a maestro in her prime

Her lesson plan went out the window
by the second week of online school
And she tempers her newfound fluidity
with a dash of Gen X cool

She doesn't know it yet
but in the years to come she will
This is what she'll be remembered for
this strange year she stayed so chill

Even when she wasn't

BACKSEAT STRIVER

Naya logged into class each day
from the backseat of her grandmother's Kia

While Abuelita delivered groceries
for Vons and Gelson's cada día

Even when it worked
the free store Wi-Fi was mostly crap

So the school loaned her out a hotspot
which Naya kept beside her lap

Princess headphones on her head
Naya worked her butt off in that car

Getting As and Bs all school year long,
second grading from afar

DYSTOPIAN NONFICTION

Julia taught Creative Writing
History and English too
But it was Dystopian Nonfiction
that left her feeling so askew

This wasn't like *The Hunger Games*
or those freaky books set in that zoo
It was real and fucking scary
and at the end you might die too

She taught strictly remotely
for a good part of the year
But the spring hybrid teaching model
filled her heart with dread and fear

Even with the new vaccine
she preferred to teach from home
But with no one to go as tribute
she dived back in alone

She didn't use a bow and arrow
but she was wise and brave and selfless
Tris Prior and Katniss strong,
even behind a mask and plastic face shield

Julia was straight-up Dauntless!

BUYING MR. G

La Reina hated homeschooling
and so did her kids
They couldn't stand Zooming
and Google Meets were the shits

The nanny stopped coming in April
the manny by mid-May
But La Reina never met a problem
that she couldn't buy away

So when school started in the fall
La Reina bought herself a teacher
And Mr. G came every day
like an old-school, small-town preacher

She paid better than the district
of that she was not vague
And Mr. G made out handsomely
while riding out the plague

REOPENING BLUES

Way down deep Bob was happy
that school was coming back
Normalcy reborn
her brand-new blue backpack

But it all seemed so sudden
it really messed with his head
And though he knew it was time
he'd rather stay in bed

There was safety in lockdown
in his cave with his clan
And rebooting this quickly
sort of fucked with his plan

But his wife and kid were so eager
shiny, excited, aglow
He just wasn't ready yet
to dad up and let them both go

I'll get there, he whispered, as they walked to school together
for the first time in 395 days

But it might take me a minute...

GENERATION COVID

PRONOUNS

He wasn't that savvy about pronouns
but she definitely tried really hard

Hanging a bright rainbow flag up
and putting that sign in their yard

His kid told her they had to move faster
get with the times, no more jokes

So he gulped down her privilege with their coffee
And did his very best to get woke

QUARANTINA COVID

Conceived during the lockdown
in her parent's living room
Quarantina COVID
had the weirdest name on Zoom

She excelled at distance learning
and history, math and art
But hated being called out or
made to stand apart

Never quite as punk rock
as her strange name would suggest
Quarantina proved most adept
at blending with the rest

She changed her name to Janet
when she turned seventeen
And married a boy who got her
Named COVID Zoom-19

They spent their years together
flattening the curve
And living for the moment
with hand wipes, masks and verve

GENERATION COVID

Kids don't always have the words
to describe just how they feel
During these truly strange, strange days
when real life is so surreal

Finding the proper language
to describe their mental anguish

Is something no school-age kid should ever have to do

And yet they did it
Every day
For a fucking year
And then some

And now they're stronger than they look
and more resilient than we know
Ready to face the world
beyond the Zoom gloom show

Resourceful as all fuck
brimming with hope and dreams and pluck

Watch out world…

Because when their time comes
to rule and roar
Generation COVID
will truly fucking soar!

COVIDIVORCE

CLEAN BREAK

She wasn't totally heartless
there were things that she would miss

But she wasn't sorry that she dumped her
even during a time like this

Being with her every day
for weeks and months on end

Showed her the hard truth of her marriage
and that it was past time to ascend

If Kelly Clarkson could do it
Demi L. and J. Lo too

The real reason for the season
might be making one from two

NINA MISSED HER STAPLER

Nina missed her office
with her windows and fancy chair
And dressing nice and wearing shoes
and fixing up her pretty hair

She missed her friends and office mates
and long lunches at that place
She even missed Barb in payroll
and that weird temp with all the lace

She missed the burnt smell of the break room
and the dull hum of computers
And her time on the train
with her fellow commuters

But more than anything…

Nina missed leaving her boyfriend at home
when she went to work
Because Jack had turned out
to be quite a jerk

She also really did miss her stapler
She loved that thing!

SPACE

He needed more space,
that's what he said
To work on himself
and get right in the head

She broke down for a bit
right after he left
But in the wild year to come
she grew far less bereft

The space he left behind
gave her more room
To rebuild and create
to blossom and bloom

And though she sometimes missed his cooking
and his goofy-dad shtick
Man, was she glad
to be rid of that prick

ALONE TIME

I know some who are suffering
locked down and alone for a year
But alone time is a pretty foreign concept
during these long-ass days around here

Thank God for headphones!

CRUEL SUMMER

TRISH'S NEW BRAND

Cute cat memes and mom jokes
were her Facebook brand online
Trish also posted food pics
when she found the time

But five months into lockdown
her brand took a hard left
Which startled Trish's newfound friends
and left her kin back home bereft

Five months of indoor living
with a world gone mad outside
Snapped poor Trish's brand wide open
and no more shit could she let slide

There would be no more likes from liars
or smiley faces from smug fucks
No feed fights with anti-maskers
with their four-wheel-drive Trump trucks

She unfriended assholes freely
and marched hard for BLM
And Trish's mom rage was contagious
just ask her husband, Jim

Her kids loved their newly woke mom too
and joined her in the fight
Masking up and hydrating
to march for what was right

MOMTIFA SOUTH

Moms bussed in from Austin,
LA and Tampa too
And some just biked on over,
Portlandians through and through

Arm in arm they made a wall
to protect the peaceful from the cops
In skinny jeans and gas masks
with bright yellow Target tops

But things did <u>not</u> go as planned

Riven by infighting
and an anti-blackness streak
The Portland Wall of Moms
barely lasted through the week

But Kiki took the lessons learned
in Portland home with her
To build a better wall of moms
that was inclusive and more fair

They were not easy conversations
there were roses and there were thorns
But by embracing their diversity
Momtifa South was born

Kiki also ditched the yellow shirts
Nobody looks good in yellow

GRACE LEE: MODEL MINORITY

Grace Lee was a model minority
her parents had taught her quite well
But even before the lockdown
she'd sensed the changing swell

They were terrorizing Asian-Americans
at her school, at the mall, on the streets
Looking for someone to scapegoat
and some model minorities to beat

When the hate fanned by Trump's bluster
left her feeling so unsafe and scared
Grace Lee simply stopped going out
and showing her face anywhere

Her parents were hurt and confused
"We are not even Chinese!"
But her Grandmother Lee remembered
dark, desperate times such as these

So they kept a low profile
stuck to home and their store
And prayed it would blow over
like yellow perils before

But as Grace Lee rode out the pandemic
her inner voice grew harder to ignore
The fire inside her was lit
and Grace Lee would be model no more

DEENA CHEN 2.0

Deena Chen hated the c-word
the one that rhymes with think
And when she heard it being used again
she didn't even blink

The time for action was upon her
so she rallied her friends around
This racist shit would not fly on her block
or anywhere else in her town

Stopping Asian hate with a single, icy glare
Deena Chen don't fuck around
cross her if you dare

Seriously, I dare you…

THE TALK

Lacretia had the talk again
with her nephews and her son
When they killed Breonna and George Floyd
and Ahmaud Arbery on his run

She used to know which points to stress
be a good kid and don't talk back
But the truth is sometimes they shoot you
just for being black

It doesn't matter if you're armed or not
or what you say or do
It's open season on black folks
and the next one could be you

And though she tries to keep it hopeful
that a brighter day is near
Experience has hardened her
and made her words more clear

Lacretia had the talk again
about young Daunte Wright
And she vows to keep on talking

And marching
And voting
And working for systemic change

Until this unholy bloodshed is made right

THE UPSIDE DOWN

THE ORANGE MENACE

He called it China virus
and sowed hatred everywhere
Severed ties with friends and allies
while bowing to Red Square

He lied about not winning
and so much other shit
And the Capitol almost crumbled
beneath the fire that he lit

The last four years have wrecked me
and chilled me to the bone
500,000 dead from COVID
on his watch alone

I like to think it's over
but you really can't tell yet
The Orange Menace is spreading
an ever-present threat

But I am ever hopeful
our better natures will prevail
When the menace fades away
like some sad, cautionary tale

THE WHITE CHAIR

Pajama Dad had a big white chair
in his young son's bedroom
Where he would sit and read to him
before the doom and gloom

He still sits there every night
and reads his pal to sleep
Trying to blot out the world
with stories, rhymes and dreams

It doesn't always work these days
and some nights sleep never comes
With worries of the day looming
like Moria's distant drums

The darkest times were in the fall
with the future so uncertain
The road ahead unmarked and dark
as the wizard's emerald curtain

But then one day in November
the torture curse was lifted
And PJ Dad rose from his chair
and felt his whole world shifted

NOVEMBER

We are at war with reality
sanity and science too
So I keep hitting refresh
hoping my guy pulls through

His number two ain't shabby either
in her pantsuits paired with Chucks
Stomping out team Big Lie's falsehoods
without giving any fucks

We really need this win right now
it feels like our last chance
So keep counting and carry on
because I'm fixing to dance!

BLUE IS THE NEW ORANGE

Banned on Twitter
Facebook too
Goodbye orange
Hello blue

MASKHOLES

TOXIC TAMMY

Tammy Talks Too Loud
went toxic by mid-summer
With hateful anti-masking screeds
that made her sound well, dumber

She lost friends and family to
the MSM's "plandemic"
But still spread her viral lies
with a hate that was endemic

To her friends not just in Burbank
but all around the country
Who lived for stoking fear and hate
in the name of living mask free

I wouldn't call it karma
but Tammy died three weeks ago
Felled by a mainstream media hoax
what a way to go!

THE WRONG HILL

If you wanna die for liberty
you should probably think it through

Dying for the right to
eat and drink
indoors
at a bar
without a mask
during a fucking pandemic
might not be your smartest move

But hey, man, you do you
bust down those swinging saloon doors
and march your manbun through

Everybody has their hill
and that MAGA bar was yours
I'll think of your last great crusade
each time I crack a Coors

Actually, probably not
I hate Coors

LATEX LARRY

Latex Larry was a producer
with two Emmys and a Globe
A first-class phony from the hills
and a massive germaphobe

He'd lived through the AIDS crisis
by playing safe and celibate
And beat back yearly colds and flus
by keeping clean as clean can get

But this shit just felt different
and left Latex Larry shook
As he locked down in the canyon
with a few hundred good books

He'd wrap himself in latex
sometimes literally all day
Even to check the mail or shoo
delivery folks away

And when the vaccine came
Larry lied to get his first
Rich prick privilege wrapped in latex
he really is the worst

LINE CUTTERS

Some said that they were doctors
others claimed to be school teachers
But most vaccine line cutters
were a-holes who were neither

So I'll take my number
and wait my turn in line
And hope karma catches up with them
sometime further down the line

I mean, seriously, haven't they ever seen a disaster movie?
Cheaters and line-cutters always die first

COVID CHRISTMAS

PAM'S (X)MAS LIST

Mark my words, Pam told her husband
I'm keeping a list
And when this shit is over
if we still exist

I'll know who our friends are
and who has done us wrong
And if we do cards again at Christmas
our list will not be that long

Especially on your side of the family

UNFRIENDED

The last thing I need
while in quarantine
Is a far-flung relation
who doesn't believe

In science or masks
or basic human rights
I'm sick of your bullshit
I'm tired of the fights

I don't care who you worship
or that you shoot and you hunt
Get the fuck off my feed
you miserable…

Huh? Oh, no, we will not be participating
in the family Christmas gift exchange this year.
Thanks, Grandma.

And, um, you're still unfriended…

SUPER-SPREADER SANTA

Lexie stayed home with her husband and kids
while her neighbors block partied outside
And caroled together while they ate and they drank
with a maskless Santa named Clyde

Lexie's kids waved from the window at their friends in the street
and Santa Clyde riding past on his sled
And though they hated their mom for keeping them home
they all spent their Christmas not dead

Clyde didn't die either but he got real sick
as did his friends down the block
But even that didn't slow down Santa Clyde's vile roll
or make him wise up and take stock

"The plandemic is a hoax and masks are for chumps!"
he screamed from his ICU bed
While Lexie and her family spent Christmas indoors
safe from Santa Clyde's super-spread

DOES THIS MASK ME LOOK FAT?

"Does this mask make me look fat?"
Alma asked as we strolled
At a distance of six feet
in the park in the cold

"Never," I lied,
because who wants to hear
How fucked we all look
at this point in the year

We're safe, we're alive
and we're just scraping by
So what harm is a little,
kind-hearted white lie?

Besides, if she really wanted to look skinny
she would have worn her black mask

SPRING AWAKENING

INAUGURATION DAY

This is a day you'll tell your kids about,
I whisper in her ear
Harris
Biden
Gorman proud
a brand-new world starts here!

Knock on wood!

WALLEY WORLD

Fatties go first
screamed the website online
Which didn't seem fair
but suited me fine

So I masked up with my kid
and drove to Walley World
To get shot number one
where the Scrambler once twirled

The park looked so surreal
overgrown and abandoned
Post-apocalyptic chic
with a vaccine site drive-in

The jab hurt a bit
but all I did was smile
A first step toward normal
after many long miles

HOPE

I have a new favorite four-letter word
and it doesn't rhyme with truck

Sometimes, even during a global pandemic
hope springs eternal

SAINT DOLLY

I don't think she's Catholic
or if that even really matters
Dolly Parton needs a sainthood
for all the good she gathers

She sings about the broken
and lonely hearts filled with regrets
Raising up the poor and the downtrodden
every single chance she gets

And now she's gone and upped her game
and helped with that new vaccine
Which might just be the saintliest thing
mine old eyes have ever seen

The unlikeliest of angels
born and bred in Tennessee
A pure-hearted backwoods Barbie
Long live sweet, Saint Dolly

AMERICAN GLOW UP

They're tearing down statues in Richmond
renaming bridges and schools in the South

Reading lists are being amended
while the old guard foams at the mouth

Changes happening every day
from sea to shining sea

The audacity of hope restored
in they/them, she/her, him/he

And I got one thing to say about that
with Pfizer shot number two in my arm

It's about fucking time!
¡Sí se puede! Sound the alarm!

But this is only the beginning
and it's nowhere near enough
We need to change the narrative
and that's where things get tough

In the meantime,
I will take Dolores Huerta Middle School
and the John Lewis Bridge
over David Starr Jordan and Edmund Pettus
any day of the fucking week

You can keep your racist team names too
a new normal is near
A post-COVID era glow up
after one truly fucked-up year

NORMAL

I'm not sure what normal looks like
on the other side of this
But I can't wait to reconnect
and laugh and hug and kiss

I dream of prime rib carving stations
at crowded weddings near and far
Dancing all night with sweaty friends
hopping from bar to bar

Fighting over game night wins
while drinking too much beer
And long road trips through red states
with no more existential fear

I'm not sure if I'll shake hands again
or fly anywhere without a mask
But, man, I sure could use a hug
you don't even have to ask

Actually, some of you should probably ask
It's been a long year and I don't know where you've been

ABOUT THE AUTHOR

Tomás Romero is an award-winning writer-producer from Los Angeles. He has written screenplays for Paramount, Sony, 20th Century Fox, Telemundo and MTV. A native of Santa Cruz, CA, Romero spent his pandemic "gap year" reading, writing, eating his feelings and perfecting his hair-cutting game with his wife and tweenage daughter in Burbank.

He also went outside a few times too.

Romero's previous poetry collection, *PTA Dad: Foul-Mouthed Poetry & Prose from a Real-Life PTA Dad*—which one reviewer described as "Witty, concise, and truthful as a kick in the nuts"—is available now from Moonbeast Media.

Made in the USA
Monee, IL
09 October 2021